M000164540

the Heavenly Habit

First published in 2017 by Columba Press
23 Merrion Square North, Dublin 2
Co. Dublin
Ireland
www.columba.ie

© 2017 Daniel O'Leary

All rights reserved. Without limiting the rights under copyright
reserved alone, no part of this publication may be reproduced,
stored in or introduced into a retrieval system, or transmitted, in
any form or by any means (electronic, mechanical, photocopying,
recording or otherwise) without the prior written permission of
both the copyright owner and the above publisher of the book.

Every effort has been made to give appropriate credit for all
material used in this book. If any involuntary infringement of
copyright has occurred, we offer our apologies and will correct
any error in future editions.

ISBN: 978-1-78218-332-7

Set in Klinic Slab Book 10/14 and Handsome Script
Book design by Alba Esteban | Columba Press
Printed by Jellyfish Solutions

IMAGE CREDITS

Front cover image by agsandrew from Shutterstock.

Photographs by Alba Esteban on pages 10, 18, 30, 34, 50,
54, 62, 102/103

Photographs from Life of Pix on pages 26, 38, 66, 68

Photographs from Unsplash on pages 24/25, 70/71, 98, 100

Photographs from Pexels on pages 14, 28, 32/33, 46, 58, 72, 74/75, 76,
80, 84, 92, 104, 108, 112, 108, 112, 114/115, 116

Painting 'Christ of St John of The Cross' by SalvadorDali, 1951.
Photograph from Kelvingrove art Gallery and Museum on page 42

Painting 'Hope' by George Frederic Watts and workshop, via
Wikimedia Commons on page 88

the Heavenly Habit

ANGELS OF THE HEART

DANIEL O'LEARY

columba press

*Dedicated to Maura, Micheál and my special
friends who, in one way or another, always find
and practice 'the heavenly habit'.*

CONTENTS

INTRODUCTION

This small book is not about Heaven; it is about Earth. Nor is it about angels; it is about mortals. It offers a key to discovering the beautiful in the most unexpected places. We hope it will brighten your life with a new and thoughtful way of considering everything, especially people, events and experiences you regard as definitely 'bad news'. The heavenly habit is that of looking at something, especially anything negative or unpleasant, in such a way that it surrenders its secret to you – the hidden goodness it carries. The old wisdom behind this belief, and it is infused into the pages of this book, is that everything has a meaning, a reason, a message – but we must search for it in a mindful, patient and positive way.

Too often we unwisely prejudge events and people at their face value. Life becomes more interesting to us, and we become more interesting to other people when we search below the negative superficialities of each day, learning something from everything, and acquiring more curious and creative minds. Developing 'the heavenly habit' of glimpsing the gold in the lead of our shadows brings the most significant transformation – personal and universal. There is a crack in every darkness – that's how the light gets in and out. And you need the darkness to discover the light. It is called the paradox of life. We are all living in it. And in there somewhere, is what we call happiness.

There is a helpful process to finding the light in the darkness. The wonderful gift of imagination plays a central role in transforming the negative into the positive, in moving from a cramped, closed and unhealthy place in your head and heart into a more free, open and delightful space. One special key to the transformation of what keeps us trapped is to visualise what we hope for, to make it present now, to feel it with our senses, to imagine ourselves being in that wonderful world of letting go of resentment, regrets or whatever our prison may be, of being free to fly. Beyond just thinking about something one desires, it is another huge step forward to be able to somehow pre-experience it, even for a moment. It is, for instance, one thing for a teacher to discuss and draw pictures, with children, of a sunny day; it is another thing entirely when they sit near the window and actually feel the warmth of the sun on their faces.

This kind of process applies to how we make the journey into the light in all 26 'habits' of the book. See the growing and healing in your thoughts and emotions as already happening. Try to become aware, in your senses, of that new freedom in your patterns of perception. This is how your goals are already becoming part of you. Know that they will be enfleshed in you when you always keep your heart open to those life-changing experiences. All great traditional wisdom knows that 'secret'. Imagine what you deeply desire for your health of heart and soul as already yours, as belonging to you, as now in your possession. And feel its presence becoming part of you.

Deepest thanks to those generous souls who accepted the challenge to help us understand those journeys from darkness to light – Adrian Scott, Brenda Pike, Christine Crabtree, Judy Roblin, Maria Bennett, Maggie Jackson, Martina Lehane Sheehan, Michael McCarthy and Theresa Wall. They have written from their hearts and in their own creative ways. Some are shy, some are apprehensive – never having been in print before, and all are brave and trusting. And just as each one is writing their reflections from where they happen to be in their own searching just now, so too each one of us, the readers, receive it from our own particular experiences and understanding of the astonishing mystery of our lives today. Deepest thanks for the work of Margaret Siberry, Martin and Maria Bennett, Andrew and Marita Thompson, Celia Sparkes, Anne Harding and Aine Moynihan; also for the guidance of Garry O'Sullivan, Michael Brennan and Alba Esteban of Columba Press.

THREE POEMS

Something of the theme of this small book is caught up by the following three poems. The first is an extract from Ralph Waldo Emerson's poem 'There alway, alway something sings':

. . . It is not only in the rose, it is not only in the bird,
not only where the rainbow glows,
nor in the song of woman heard.
But in the darkest, meanest things
there alway, alway, something sings.

'Tis not in highest stars alone, nor in the cups of
*   budding flowers,*
nor in the red-breast's mellow tone,
nor in the bow that smiles in showers:
but in the mud and scum of things,
there alway, alway, something sings.

(RALPH WALDO EMERSON – 1803–1882.

THE COMPLETE WORKS 1904, VOL IX. POEMS)

The second reflective poem 'The Guest House' also catches the spirit of this book. It is written by the wonderful Persian poet Rumi:

This human being is a guest-house;
every morning a new arrival;

a joy, a depression, a meanness –
some momentary awareness comes
as an unexpected visitor.

Welcome and entertain them all!
Even if they're a crowd of sorrows,
who violently sweep your house
empty of all your furniture;
still treat each guest honourably.
He may be clearing you out for some new delight.

The dark thought, the shame, the malice –
meet them at the door laughing,
and invite them in.

Be grateful for whoever comes,
because each has been sent
as a guide from beyond.

(JALALUDDIN RUMI, RUMI – SELECTED POEMS, *TRANS*
COLEMAN BARKS WITH JOHN MOYNCE, A. J. ARBERRY,
REYNOLD NICHOLSON: PENGUIN BOOKS, 2004.)

The third poem, 'The Quilt' (unpublished), is something I wrote to help me understand the complexity of our lives, especially how the light and darkness of our experiences are intertwined. It may help us to explore more deeply the mystery of our being.

As they say it does
Just before I died, like a small ocean
my life flattened into a wavy
patchwork quilt

Just before they went glassy, as they say they do
my eyes suddenly saw everything clearly
and at the completion of the last stitch
they understood the whole complex interweaving

My darkest times were now the brightest patches
and the 'sinful' pieces held them all together.
The weakest patterns came from my proudest
    moments
and my deeds of goodness
were the most threadbare of all

The finest colours, I learned
were mixed at twilight, without permission;
and the shapes of beauty, only now so clear,
were drawn with my left hand –
wild and pagan

And then I saw a shy and shining thread of gold
(and remembered telling it in confession) ‿
a moment that was unknowingly divine …
And as they say it does, a secret was revealed to me –
the light in the dark of mystery

ALPHABET OF ANGELS

A – Anxiety to Peace: MICHAEL MCCARTHY

B – Bitterness to Contentment: DANIEL O'LEARY

C – Criticism to Praise: CHRISTINE CRABTREE

D – Darkness to Light: CHRISTINE CRABTREE

E – Envy to Rejoicing: MARTINA LEHANE SHEEHAN

F – Fear to Bravery: MARIA BENNETT

G – Grief to Acceptance: BRENDA PIKE

H – Hatred to Freedom: MAGGIE JACKSON

I – Idleness to Passion: MARTINA LEHANE SHEEHAN

J – Judgement to Appreciation: BRENDA PIKE

K – Kitsch to Authentic: JUDY ROBLIN

L – Loss to Growth: BRENDA PIKE

M – Miserly to Magnanimous: THERESA WALL

ANXIETY TO PEACE

Most people, most days, carry anxiety of some kind. Young and old, at all levels of society, are admitting to panic attacks, fits of depression and significant degrees of stress. The amount of prescribed medication has doubled in ten years. Mindfulness apps and 'talking therapies' are in huge demand. Much of our anxiety lies below our conscious awareness. It is a silent destroyer of happiness. It corrodes our inner peace. From within our fragile spirit this darkness emerges. Sometimes it is triggered by our own inner and fearful insecurity, sometimes for other reasons: there is no escaping the 24/7 disturbing media news that bombards our homes and hearts. Even the strong-minded, positive and successful people are not immune. People long to be free from their mental prisons. Michael McCarthy remembers a beautiful moment of grace.

Michael writes: In 2012 I spent three months as Writer in Residence in the unit for stroke and dementia at Tallaght Hospital, Dublin. The fruit of the residency was a poetry collection called *The Healing Station,* named after a set of sculptures in the hospital chapel by the artist Anna Duncan depicting six healing miracles from St Luke's Gospel.

The title was a metaphor for what happened daily in the hospital, the dedication of staff in the face of tiny increments of improvement. I learned to watch for small moments of epiphany. The incident here occurred the day before I was invited to contribute to this publication.

Taking Communion to Jennifer

I find her in good form.
We chat awhile, then move on to prayer.
Today her responses are clear and immediate.
As we make our way through the Our Father
I sense a presence in the space behind me.
Concentrating on the moment, I continue:
Lord I am not worthy that you should enter
Under my roof ... As she receives the host
A warm breath caresses the back of my neck.
Turning, I see an elderly resident in slippers,
Her face stricken. A single sob escapes from her.
Placing a hand on her forehead I say the blessing.
Her full-on smile radiates down the length of my arm.
Something is unlocked in us.

MICHAEL MCCARTHY

BITTERNESS TO CONTENTMENT

Bitterness has a sharp edge to it; it cuts deep into the soul; it spreads poison in hearts. While something can be said for anger, fear, guilt – bitterness is graceless. It is a dark room with no light. It takes a long healing. For many it is a curse of the second half of the hurt life. Those who pay attention to the state of their souls may be blessed with a glimpse of this subtle, destructive emotion and catch it in time. It may begin with unfavourable family wills, betrayals, missed opportunities because of gossip, ill-will, or jealousy. Or it can arise from a sense of unfairness, injustice or false accusations.

Holding on to bitterness ends all real growing or blossoming. It is an immense and impossible weight. New desires and possibilities cannot be discerned if all our energy is consumed in a shrunken negativity. Can the condition ever be healed? Only by love – a moment of true affection. Or a sudden and intense experience can open the shutters and shock the sick soul. This may be the beginning. Salvation follows. This new freedom for creativity, and the new surge of energy is pure redemption. The path ahead is thrown open. The possibilities, then, are endless.

Invisible blight on every plant;
A sprinkled poison ends all growing.
A curse that kills, no harvest happens,
Until a grace redeems the sowing.

DANIEL O'LEARY

CRITICISM TO PRAISE

When you hear an idea, or watch a performance, are you quick to see its shortcomings? Do you respond, 'It was okay, but …'? Perhaps this makes you feel you are discerning, when all the while you are critical. The person involved goes away disheartened that they are so far short of the mark.

Develop instead a habit of encouragement. When you are shown something, find something to praise, however small. Even if it is only that the person has put a lot of hard work into it, thank them for it. Find ways of acknowledging their gifts. When you practise this approach, you learn to see more things that you can praise, and you find yourself giving thanks naturally and fully. Praise becomes more of a habit than criticism ever was.

You also find that you become more patient with your own shortcomings, and more likely to accept that what you offer is more than good enough: is your own unique gift to those around you – and that, too, is a reason to give thanks.

A calculated put-down might seem clever,
But words of praise will last for ever.

CHRISTINE CRABTREE

DARKNESS TO LIGHT

Do you ever feel to be in the dark, with no sense of an end to it, no sign of light dawning? Bulbs need to be planted if they are ever to germinate. They wait in our autumn gardens' deep darkness for the midwife touch of spring. We cannot simply plant the bulbs when we want instant flowers; there is nature's necessary life-giving sleep of gestation. Then, at the right time, the bulb begins to send up shoots and we can look forward to spring flowers. The bulb has been prepared in the dark to produce something beautiful.

So it is when we ourselves are in the dark. We long to escape this darkness and come into the light again. But during the time we are in the dark, important things are going on. While our ego tells us we are lost and alone, and that there will be no end to the darkness, our true self is being honed by the experience so that it will be ready to come to the fore at the right time – and blossom. Without the gift of darkness, in fact, we would never truly see!

In the dark, preparation:
New shoots come, jubilation:
Spring in my winter, celebration!

CHRISTINE CRABTREE

ENVY TO REJOICING

'Great, we are up near the front', we giggled, as we sat behind the seats marked 'reserved' (for some dignitaries, we presumed). Just as the concert began and the lights were lowered, a steward arrived quietly, torch in hand. Taking down the reserved signs from the seats in *front of us*, she whispered 'Here ye are lads, these haven't been taken, so ye can sit here.' 'Huh', I muttered, '*they*, arrived later than us, yet got better seats.' Lips pursed, arms folded, I sat seething behind their gleeful bobbing heads.

What was it the vineyard owner said to those envious of the latecomers? 'Why be envious because I am generous?' (Mt 20: 16). A little ashamed, I unlocked my tightly folded arms and opened them even further later on – when I received a surprise bottle of wine in the raffle! Life's Gospel vineyard-keeper seemed to wink.

Green is the colour of envy, but also the colour of growth; maybe it lets us know when our vision has narrowed; when our ripe grapes are rotting, unpicked from the vine. Maybe it nudges us towards a bigger place, just a breath away, where there is enough for everyone.

Generous Vine-keeper, Lover, Rejoicer,
Wildly abundant towards the last and the first,
Giver of life, transform our sour grapes
Into sweet flowing wine.

MARTINA LEHANE-SHEEHAN

FEAR TO BRAVERY

Fear is often an unwillingness to let go of the tried and trusted, or to speak out in case it rocks the boat. Fear can lock the sufferer into an impasse leading to a form of superstition that things will go wrong if anything changes. There is transformation of the frightened self when we face and feel the fear – and still continue trustingly and bravely towards the wished-for goal.

One route to freedom from fear is to know that change does not mean the loss of anything essential or dear to us; rather, what once was part of us is transformed, but still present; the appearance may alter but the essence, enhanced by new experience and perspective, will remain. In our own efforts to die to our fears, the truth of who we already are begins to blossom. There is no sudden replacement of any part of our given humanity. The seeds are already there. They need to be nourished and cherished for the 'false self' to die into the 'true self'.

The green glass vase will break in transit
so smash it now;
either you will try to carry your memento,
and it will crack,
or you will refuse to leave it behind and never travel;

broken is the only way to carry the vase,
each piece a doll's house saucer of light,
each a palm open
to the room where you pack to leave.

Beat the light into crystals
so that you are free to move –
and when you travel,
fold them in a cloth.

At your destination,
don't try to reassemble the vase;
its old form has gone –

but in the workshop at the lough-side
tip out the crushed pieces
and fuse them into something new.

MARIA BENNETT

Author's Note: The green glass vase is an object of
importance. The poet explores the idea that if the
'you' to whom the poem is addressed hangs on to
the vase and is afraid of it breaking, there will be
no possibility of travel or change.

GRIEF TO ACCEPTANCE

The white-knuckle ride of grief! To be cast adrift on an unexpected roller-coaster, never knowing where you are going to be, or when, with no control over the sudden journey of mourning, how to end it. Fighting it, resisting it just causes more pain and frustration. Nature has its own healing way. You learn that strapping yourself in for the unavoidable journey of letting go is the only option. But the river is rough and the mourners on the banks of it are full of aching memories and desperate loss. Wave after wave of peaks and troughs of intense emotion reach to engulf me. How can I believe anything in this situation? 'If you trust the river of life,' Krishnamurti wrote, 'the river of life has an astonishing way of taking care of you'. I will not drown, sink, be abandoned, die of grief. One day I will know that there is no real separation. Even after death, love grows. I name my journey 'Acceptance of the Seas'.

Embrace the blessed unrest;
The hollowing and hallowing;
The emptying and the filling.
The dawn froth and spume of surface waves
Have messages to teach us.

Greet and welcome them for
They bring to you the alchemy of grief.
A 'knowing without knowing', deep as the oceans,
With its own lovely light to guide us to another place.

BRENDA PIKE

HATRED TO FREEDOM

I think of Titian's painting *Ecce Homo* (Behold the Man), which depicts Jesus, tortured and ridiculed, a very mortal victim. But I also think of Salvador Dalí's *Christ of St John of the Cross*, where Christ hangs unbound on the cross to which hatred nailed him on Earth. His body is now youthful and strong. He is free to show humanity that nothing, not even the most cruel and extreme acts of hatred, can keep us from experiencing the freedom from anguish and pain that is eternally offered by a loving God.

But a future eternity isn't the exclusive province of heaven. William Blake saw infinity in the palm of his hand and 'eternity in an hour'. If I choose not to be bound and blinded by hatred, eternal freedom can be found right here, right now, in my choice to be an embodiment of God's love.

My poem 'The Acrobat' is a reflection on Dalí's painting which makes visible the divinely human capacity for transformation.

See him, the Beloved,
the accomplished acrobat,
poised now, impossibly,
on his celestial trapeze,

muscles rippling
with supreme strength.

Having stretched his skill
to the limits of earth,
walked the tightrope of
belief and unbelief,
and tumbled chaotically
through the chasms of death,
he leaps across the universe
like Solomon's gazelle.

This final somersault
leaves humanity gasping.

MAGGIE JACKSON

IDLENESS TO PASSION

'The devil finds work for idle hands', many of us were told, and we still believe it. Feeling guilty for being idle, we employ the inner critic to justify us, or to beat us into action, and, of course, we end up with even more inertia. You know what it's like on those days when you start off with huge expectations of yourself, but you gradually become so overwhelmed you end up doing nothing. Inertia then freezes your heart like a block of ice. 'Ah, couldn't be bothered', you eventually tell yourself, as you slump into idleness, burying your fear (and your passion), and putting life out of reach for yourself.

Only when we apply the soothing balm of truth and compassion, can our tired excuses begin to melt. Yes, the medicine is in the wound – which must be named, not shamed. What is its name? Is it fear, low self-esteem, sloth? The dread exposure of being a frightened beginner? Maybe we are not just lazy, maybe we are terrified. What if we could just place our frail little hand into a Bigger, Guiding Hand, and take one small step, and then another. Even if, with unsure steps and wobbly knees, we can remember that the rest of those real (or imagined) sceptical onlookers, begrudgers, braggers and criticisers are also, secretly, just resistant and maybe terrified beginners themselves. Wake up to your own amazing grace or your soul may never stir itself to participate in the dance we call life, in the passionate quest for which we were created.

Shedding coats of dead routines,
A frightened soul uncurls, uncoils,
Tender wound reveals the seed –
Life's longing for itself.

MARTINA LEHANE-SHEEHAN

JUDGEMENT TO PRAISE

There is an unhappy place in most of us that is patterned into habits of criticism, blame and judgement. It is the silent shadow of the small soul. It makes true happiness impossible. You cannot be free to genuinely rejoice with the success of others, with the happiness of your colleagues, while the fingers of jealousy and negativity clutch your slow and brooding heart. At every moment we have a choice; do we opt for the stingy and belittling view of what is happening, or for the opening of our hearts to a finer, expansive vision; do we applaud, support, delight in what is good, true and beautiful? What useless, self-harming grievance can I resist today? And what life-giving, soul-expanding blessing can I invoke on the fullness of each one's struggling life, of each community's commitment to the common good? Without the bigger picture of the living Love that creates, sustains and guides all things to their final harvest, the human stain of blind resistance will blight the dreams. Only the birds will sing the Creator's praise. 'Like them', wrote Schubert, 'I want to die from singing'.

May I plead for different eyes to look
Beyond the horizon of vulnerable human sight

To the really Real, to the love-energy within Creation.
To see the reflected face of the Creator in
The countenance of the stranger, in the eye of the
    mayfly,
In the mysteries of space. To recognise, even in the
    cruelties and evils
Of our evolving world and its humanity, the
    unrestrainable, irrepressible
Search for Love.

BRENDA PIKE

KITSCH TO AUTHENTIC

A visiting holy man began his talk with a question: 'How would you feel if I told you that God thinks you are wonderful, and that he is head-over-heels in love with you'? A lone voice replied, 'Sceptical!' People laughed because, I suspect, that was how most of them felt too. But reflect for a moment on how exciting that might be. To be loved like that by the Creator-Mother of all beauty! All that is needed is to respond with a personal 'Yes', a delighted acceptance of this astonishing truth. And yet, full of doubt, we hold back. Is there a loving Creator? How can I, a pretty useless individual, be worthy of that kind of relationship? Others may be afraid of their own potential to change the world; they resist accepting their own gifts and talents, their own attractiveness and power.

They fail to grow into the fullness that they are created for, into the people they are called to be. Growing is too risky, dreaming is too dangerous; easier to stay in the shadows and peep through the curtained windows of life. But the light and fire in us must be released. What we lack is the courage to believe in our own authenticity, our own inner authority. Once we set out to become our true selves all kinds of power are released in our hearts. To be fully alive! If you do not live life, life will live you.

There is a hidden seed in your heart waiting to blossom into its true beauty, waiting for the touch of love from the Creator who is in love with you. As this wee book keeps insisting, without the darkness this hidden seed will never see the light!

And Love waits with patience
As a mother does the birth of her child,
Loving from the beginning
What is still waiting to be born.

JUDY ROBLIN

LOSS TO GROWTH

There are paradoxes at every moment of our lives, in every line we write. The shadows of life hold the key to our growing and understanding. Without loss there can be no true abundance. We grow by subtraction. It is only in the night that we can see the stars. Without the dank, cold soil around the seed there will be no bountiful harvest. We ourselves often need replanting in the fallow fields of our desire for new roots and new shoots to bless, purify and heal our hearts. And then the pain! There is always the pain! Even the truest love brings the greatest suffering. If you dare to love be prepared to grieve. Only the winter of the greatest love and the greatest suffering combine to bring the slow beginning to the dying seed. The unbearable wound of loss can never be banished; it can only gradually be loved into the ever-green hope, vision and freedom of the blossoming heart.

Body in a chair; brain in a whirl.
Is this what growing old is?
Stagnant, stuck, lost.
The future is a cold mist.
Is it foolish to speak of learning the final lesson
With humour and dogged courage?

To offer the blank mornings that promise more
    diminishments,
Relinquishments and losses
As the day's worship?

BRENDA PIKE

MISERLY TO 'MAGNANIMOUS'

When we sift with honesty through the delicate web of our daily lives, we find that our attitudes are often manifested in self-protection and a kind of hoarding. We stifle the natural generosity of the soul in the mistaken and miserly belief that by conserving our love, and cosily defining its boundaries, our personal treasure-house of proud virtue remains intact. It is easy to dispense our love with a false egoism, carefully counting the cost and fearfully tidying the receipts into our impressive filing system, safely constructed over the closed windows of our souls. This diminishes the very gift we seek to protect, for love can only flourish and be itself by a continual reaching out, expanding and freely overflowing into all the crazy and varied dimensions of creation – human and non-human. We only ever truly keep what we give away. Pope Francis asks whether we act out of our *anima magna* (our 'magnanimous' soul) or our *anima pusilla* (our miserly soul)? And Pope John XXIII said, *See everything, overlook a lot, correct a little, bless all.* This is only ever possible when we surrender to Love.

No threat to step beyond the known
into the darkness of union;

for all is love
and in this vast creation
there are arms enough
to embrace,
enfold
and multiply
the eternal beats of this great heart.
So I surrender – there is no other way.

THERESA WALL

NEGATIVE TO ENTHUSIASTIC

Grumpy, negative people are not particularly popular. Our moods affect others. Our hearts are made for shining, and people catch that light off us. Do you sometimes notice how many of your thoughts and emotions are damaging and cynical? That is a good start. Try to avoid judging, blaming, criticising and resenting; they drain your very being. 'Years wrinkle the skin,' said Samuel Ullman, 'but to give up enthusiasm wrinkles the soul'. Once you learn how to drop old jealousies, old scores, old hurts, then you find a deeper and more fulfilling life. This will be a struggle for you – but the rewards are such a blessing. A healthy and vibrant enthusiasm is achieved by letting go of those deep-rooted attitudes and negative habits of the mind. It takes much courage to find and follow the light that emerges from the darkness. Remember that to be 'enthused' is to be God-filled, to be divinised, to be in-toxicated by the Holy Spirit. 'In the middle of my winter', wrote the poet, 'I found an invincible summer.'

> Rake the muck this way, rake the muck that way, it
>   will still be muck:
> Reach for the light, dance in your heart – or forever
>   stay stuck.

DANIEL O'LEARY

OVER-CAUTIOUS TO RISKING

Were your parents over-cautious? Do you always care-fully observe the rules? Are you known for 'playing it safe'? At certain times you may have good reasons for behaving in such a manner. But without taking risks, fol-lowing your heart from time to time, you cannot blossom and grow into your true self. If your motto is *carpe diem*, the desire to live life to the hilt, then there will be many mistakes, but a deeper satisfaction and sense of fulfil-ment. If you do not risk failure, and maybe even being ridiculed or humiliated, then you just cannot delight in discovery, or celebrate your own authority and authen-ticity. The compulsion to be always right, to remain in 'the state of grace', to be forever safe, is a deadly block to your creative urge, your delightful imagination. Without the break-down of your rigid defences, there will be no break-through of your desire to be flying and free. We become ill when we deny our deepest instinct. There is a force within us that needs to be always reaching for what is beyond us, to be for ever compelled to explore, to take the risk of discovering what's over the next mountain.

So give me every time,
The hottest sinner or the half-mad saint.
But gods and fallen angels please protect me
From those 'middle-people' whose hearts are faint.

DANIEL O'LEARY

PITY TO EMPATHY

'Back on the drink again; the likes of you are a real pity,' I said under my breath. 'Why can't you just get it together?' You are looking at me with an expression that does not reach your eyes. I don't want to reach your eyes either. I feel strangely awkward, maybe even afraid. 'No,' I argue vehemently with myself, 'I am not like you. I have nothing to hide. My life is an open book. And I'm always in control of it'.

Walking on stilts on the slippery slope of denial is a tiring thing, but its hard to tell you the reason. What if you knew that, very often, and secretly, I too cannot 'get it to-gether'. My life too is unmanageable whenever I am in the grip of doing it 'my ego's way', clinging to the certitudes of my false self, trying to control the uncontrollable. Ah! but my busy-ness, possessions, privilege, and worshipping at altars of reputation and success are such hidden compul-sions – the accepted addictions in society!

I pause. I notice my shallow defences, and somehow a silent communication passes between us. Something in me shivers. 'Yes, you are me, I am you; when you limp, I limp; when you exhale, I inhale, because we are all exqui-sitely joined in the one breath'. And we all drink from the one well. It is not so much 'There but for the grace of God go I', but rather 'There go I'.

God grant me the serenity to accept the speck in my
   brother's eye.
Courage to see the plank in my own
And compassion to embrace us both

MARTINA LEHANE-SHEEHAN

There's a coward in all of us; there's a hero in all of us. 'Tis a strange truth but this contradiction lives in the heart of every human being – even those we admire and follow. There is a story about the two wolves who are forever fighting in all our souls – the wolf of menace and evil; the wolf of harmony and energy. And who wins? The one you feed! The one you befriend each day. When things are not looking too good, risk opening your heart to befriend the wolf of courage. The prize is priceless. You find the heroine within; the leader you were born to become. All you seek is already within you. You are made in the image of your Creator. Your truest self is a small flame waiting to burn with immense power and influence. In 1875 William Ernest Henley wrote his famous 'Invictus'. It begins,

Out of the night that covers me
Black as the pit from pole to pole
I thank whatever gods may be
For my unconquerable soul.

QUILLER-COUCH, ARTHUR THOMAS (ED.) THE OXFORD
BOOK OF ENGLISH VERSE: 1250–1900, *CLARENDON*
PRESS, 1902, P. 1019.

When you believe in your immense potential then everything is possible. That is the purpose of your life, the reason you were born. The quaking is over. Begin to see yourself in a new light. The darkness will be heavy; the struggle will be a daily one. And the dawn is very near.

It's up to you; you have the choice;
to stay asleep or throw the dice.
To play it safe and then to die
or trust your heart – and fly!

DANIEL O'LEARY

REJECTED TO BELONGING

To move from Rejection to Belonging takes a courageous transformation, and perhaps some small measure of Mother Julian's certainty that 'All shall be well.' Sometimes the harsher or more unjustified the rejection, the fiercer and more essential the need to belong becomes. The absence of somewhere or someone to belong to feels like an unbearable loss, and can be utterly dispiriting. Rejection kills something in us. Since we are all born to love and be loved, rejection is the deepest pain. It closes too many doors of healing and growing. But once we belong again, the sense of being 'home', being loved and wanted, is life-giving. The new home, community, relationship, or outlook might be unexpected but it is recognisable in the deepest part of our souls. We were born to belong.

The first step in this growing into belonging is the sense of belonging to ourselves. This is not always easy. The first step in making headway and heart-way along this path of self-respect and self-esteem is to believe that we are unconditionally and personally loved by the God we believe in. Only then will our existential fear be transformed by divine, extravagant love experienced in the loving community.

When I experienced a painful rejection (from my community) I had a recurring dream about Cappadocia – somewhere I'd never been. My poem 'Cappadocia' exemplifies my yearning to belong and find home.

Cappadocia.
Its sound beckons me:
'Come back', 'Come soon.'
So I search maps and books,
trying to pinpoint the place of my dreams.

Cappadocia.
The name sings to me
like notes from childhood poems –
Nineveh,
Avalon,
The Isles of the Blessed.

How can I see a house I must enter,
with its door opening
and someone I know to be my beloved,
smiling, open-armed,
eager to embrace?

MAGGIE JACKSON

STRESSED-OUT TO BREAK-THROUGH

We live with stress, it becomes habitual, a dark companion. Peace is more elusive; it requires a kind of work, an active seeking. But seeking is met by finding, a balm's breath.

The phone rings, the list grows,
the fluorescent light flickers over
the ruthless screen, eating time.
The traffic is heavier than I hoped,
the hospital queue stretches into
a future prickling with uncertainty.
Please say she passed and that
one of the layers of worry that I wear
can be shed like an old skin.
When will the news be good
instead of this constant bracing
against the oncoming austerity?
And there is the old enemy, the tightening
of the knot that was once a stomach,
the scars of anxieties' track marks.
Then you see the liver-spotted hand
reaching across the tubes and wires
assuaging fear with fifty years of love.

Twenty-Four Hours in A&E, just TV
to take me to sleep, to soften the sore
muscles of uphill stone wrangling.
'I don't want you to leave me'
says one octogenarian to another,
'life is nothing without you'.
My hand reaches across the sofa
to the one that took mine at an altar,
one squeeze is balm to my stress.
We are a home to each other,
a shelter, a respite, a redoubt,
sensed under the skin of a long day.

ADRIAN SCOTT

TIMID TO CONFIDENT

The pain of timidity can lead to an incapacity to participate in life, can lock the sufferer away so that the excitement of learning and making mistakes is lost to them. Its root can be insidious, might come from fear, embarrassment or shame, or be due to repression by others; but the outcome is always the same in that the sufferer will sense that they are missing out on life. Timidity can breed further timidity.

This doesn't mean that to be away from the busyness of life or to be content is wrong, but growth and development is natural, and timidity can abort this. There is something wonderful in witnessing the confidence and the dawning realisation of the possible in the once timid person as they become willing to take chances in and on life.

Broken Lyre
You cannot see her
for the soft blue of the firmament—
she dresses to be lost,
slow dances the turning earth,
takes refuge in the pluck
of a single string.

Draw closer, pick out the harm—
a rip through sleeve to skin;
note how she does not flinch
leans toward the denouement.

MARIA BENNETT

....

Author's Note: 'Broken Lyre', inspired by a paint-
ing called Hope *by George Frederic Watts, in*
which a blindfolded woman sits on a globe holding
a lyre with only one string, portrays the woman
as wishing to disappear, 'dressing to be lost'. The
poem finishes, however, by portraying the woman
bravely facing whatever is coming to her in life,
She does not draw away but 'leans toward ...'

UNDESERVING TO BLESSED

The epidemic of low self-esteem haunts us. We carry around the gnawing doubt about our own goodness. Blessings are ordinary moments seen with the eyes of grace.

I put their leads on full of begrudging,
the rain is audible even through the door
and the winter light is already fading.
The young collie yanks the lead
of my dissatisfaction, a reminder that
I failed to attend to his daily training.
We face the wind, heads leaning into
the onrushing erosion of the blown wetness
seeming to deem us undeserving of any grace.
Up the cloddy path sticking to my boots,
an indictment, each squelching step
another evidence of my poor progress.
Coming around the stone-built cottages
and up the ginnel, funnelling the three dogs
into a yelping clutter under my tetchy feet.
Out of sorts, isn't that what they call it,
when the world you find meets all the
low expectations you carried into it?
Then we reach the head of the valley,

whittling the broken end of my tether,
only to look up as the clouds break.
The great orb of the low sun gleams
from behind the leaf shorn beech tree
and we all stop as if music were playing.
The lost Eden opens its generous gates
to animal and human, we pass through
into momentary, unsought beatitude.

ADRIAN SCOTT

VINDICTIVE TO FORGIVING

The sting of criticism, the wounds we are heir to, leave us disgruntled, even angry. This festers and makes us smaller than we are. Forgiveness expands the heart and creates room for life.

Unbelievable, I have become chained
to the radiator of your unwillingness
to address the issues that hold us captive.
I cannot escape the facts of your life
the way you seem able to, and then pin
all the responsibility on me, or anyone.
What is stopping you from facing it all,
for God's sake, literally, and for mine,
your inaction is like a terrorist cell.
I am an angry hostage, meekened by fear,
yet seething at the injustice of my plight,
strangely enamoured by my captivity.
And then you turn out of that mood
into the prodigal's return, not a
long trudge but a swift change of weather.
My maintenance of a suitable distance
that doesn't reek of co-dependence,
is dissolved by your unstudied vulnerability.

Your return, yet again from the far country,
the place of squandered inheritance,
is an affront to my sense of rightness.
Yet I feel deeper plates sliding apart
revealing another reality, contrary
to all the rational balance sheet tallies.
It is the power of my love for you
that issues from a secret storage
and reveals itself at that rooftop sighting.
It is the running down the street,
arms wide open, ridiculous prodigality
of heart gashing, faith in forgiveness.

ADRIAN SCOTT

WOUNDED TO HEALER

In Oscar Wilde's story 'The Selfish Giant'' Christ, in the form of a small child, tells the Giant who is outraged at seeing the child's scarred hands, that 'These are the wounds of love.' It's a very human revelation for the Giant, an awakening that heals him from his own wounds of selfishness, and then enables him to heal and love others.

My poem 'A Hunslet Peace' (extract below) describes how a small girl dug up some flowers I had planted and moved them to sunnier, more fertile ground. My misunderstanding of what I assumed was an act of theft or vandalism made me feel wounded. I wanted to find the culprit and voice my anger. But I later saw the flowers flourishing as they were tended by the child and my anger dissolved into tears of gratitude for her innocent act of kindness. My own wounds healed as we became gardeners together, and, since then, as I share the poem with people, I become a healer too.

Having no language we could share,
we wordlessly dug and watered;
moving anger from its mulch of darkness,
changing judgement into fertile kindness,
soaking the soil with tears of forgiveness,
grafting joy onto a Hunslet terrace,
and rooting peace between two united hearts.

MAGGIE JACKSON

X-RATED TO GOLD

'Today is the day' was the mantra of Mel Fisher, a professional underwater treasure-hunter who searched the Florida Keys for fifteen years before finding the Spanish galleon he was seeking all his life. It is a good mantra. It is full of expectancy and a positive mind-set. It believes in possibility. Today can 'be the day' for us too, when we begin afresh each morning our search for the treasure we seek that lies deep in the ocean of our own hearts. The key is to believe. We cannot have shining eyes, a determined heart if we regard ourselves as unimportant, unworthy and unattractive. To live each day at a time is a golden aim, and to live it with a gentle confidence, no matter what mistakes, failures and disappointments we encounter in our lives. Believing we are unconditionally loved, the eyes of our hearts will learn to recognise the hidden treasures strewn all around us. Everything will begin to shine with the gold of Spirit. Even within all that is x-rated in our lives, in our world, there is the paradox of healing, renewal and transformation. (Note the Ralph Waldo Emerson poem in the Introduction.) That's what this little book is really about – beginning to understand that it is in the heart of darkness the light is born, from the abyss of our wound the new strength emerges, and, as W. B. Yeats wrote, 'in the desert of the heart let the healing fountain start'.

> *There is no path.*
> *The path is made as we walk with*
> *Pebbles carried from the wild places of life*
> *With bruised hearts and bleeding fingers guiding us*
>   *home*
> *To the divine destination of ourselves.*

JUDY ROBLIN

YOU, THE FALSE SELF – TO YOU, THE TRUE SELF

Your False Self is most probably the self you think you are! It is not a bad self. It is your small self, still under-nourished, still shallow, still petty and touchy. It is imprisoned by the trappings of the ego – your body image, your job, your education, success and ambition – and your attachment to these. The False Self is what changes, passes and dies when you die. Only your True Self lives forever. The whole point of Life's quest is to lead you to an experience of your True Self. It is the purpose of religion, of salvation – that the immortal diamond of your deepest, most real and authentic self begins to shine. You are becoming love.

Mystic Thomas Merton writes of the True Self: 'Then it was as if I suddenly saw the secret beauty of their hearts, the depths of their souls where neither sin nor desire nor self-knowledge can reach, the core of their reality, the person that each is in God's eyes.' There is a part of you that has always said 'yes' to God, that is always in complete oneness with the divine flow, a music in perfect pitch with the melody of heaven's heart. This is your divine DNA, your inner destiny, that absolute core that is always intimate with the heart of God. All your life you have two companions vying for your attention – your big and beautiful Self, your small and anxious Self. Have you made your choice?

> *Yet again you are trudging into the dark weather*
> *Of your mind. Your eyes are dull. Your*
> *Heart heavy with too many things.*
> *A stranger is keeping in step with you. His*
> *Face is beautiful with love. You look away.*
> *You look back again. He's gone. And then you know.*
> *It was a glimpse of your truest, faithful self.*

DANIEL O'LEARY

ZERO TO ZENITH

Sometimes it is all in the seeing, in the waiting, in the not-rushing-to-judge. Harry was a drop-out alcoholic who lived in a dilapidated caravan site on the other side of town. It was a small but pathetic community separated from the prosperous post-codes of the city by a screen of squalid surroundings – a place of no beauty. A leg ulcer prevented Harry from walking and I was sent as a social worker to help him with basic needs. Like all the residents on the site, Harry had seen better days, and the dire circumstances of his life now were bordering on the below-human level of acceptability. Dull and damaged, he was seen, and saw himself, as a worthless failure, someone to be avoided, or be got rid of. But we stayed true to Harry. We believed in the gold in the rubble, the light in his darkness, the spark in the ashes. There was a transformation. Harry's spirit slowly began to soar like a bird. Our love was setting him free to believe in himself again, to remember how to laugh out loud, to taste a lost joy. We went to his funeral. He was buried with full military honours. Unknown to us, Harry was a hero. We thought of Harry's caravan site. And his lonely life in the wrong side of town. And his greatest shining moment when he realised he was loved.

And it's here that I find you
Who turns the world upside down,
As heaven's delight is loosed
By you – a beggar of beauty.

JUDY ROBLIN

IN THEIR OWN WORDS . . .

ADRIAN SCOTT:

'I am a 56-year-old poet, husband, father, dog walker. I live in the Rivelin Valley, Sheffield, a place where steel was first sharpened. I spend much of my time trying to sharpen words so that they pierce the heart.'

BRENDA PIKE:

'Nurse, midwife, wife (of an Anglo-Catholic priest), mother, widow: and also, a child of the universe, an image of the mystery of Being, a drop in the ocean of love, interconnected with all creatures of the one unfathomable Source. Kept, held, loved unutterably.'

CHRISTINE CRABTREE:

'I am a Methodist minister who has found ideas such as are contained in this book to be life-changing, and I'm still trying to take in that I'm loved to the uttermost.'

DANIEL O'LEARY:

'I continue to be amazed at the mysteries of nature and grace, of creation and incarnation. I wish we had been told these beautiful and life-changing stories when we were young. *An Astonishing Secret: The Love-Story of Creation and the Wonder of You* is just published.'

JUDY ROBLIN:

'I am a mother and grandmother living with my husband on the west coast of Wales. I enjoy the surprise of discovering what is extraordinarily hidden within ordinary daily living, whilst witnessing its reflection in the wild wonder of nature around me.'

MAGGIE JACKSON:

'I am a Youth Worker and now a Spiritual Director, Retreat Guide, Poet and aspiring novelist. My writing career began at the age of six when I won a national competition on the theme of 'Chocolate'!'

MARIA ISAKOVA BENNETT:

'I work as a teacher, artist and poet; collaborate on projects in galleries on Merseyside; and was recently awarded a Northern Writers' Award. I create and co-edit, with Michael Brown, a stitched poetry journal, *Coast to Coast to Coast*. I have a new pamphlet forthcoming with Eyewear in autumn 2017.'

MARTINA LEHANE SHEEHAN:

'I am an Accredited Psychotherapist, Spiritual Director and Retreat Facilitator. I direct retreats and workshops in many countries. My fourth book, *Surprised by Fire*, is now available. (See www.corkwellbeingcounselling.ie)

MICHAEL MCCARTHY:

'I'm a priest in Sherburn in Elmet in the Diocese of Leeds. I'm also a spiritual director, and have published three collections of poetry. My most recent collection, *The Healing Station*, published by The Poetry Business, is the fruit of a writing residency at a unit for stroke and dementia at Tallaght Hospital, Dublin.'

THERESA WALL:
'I studied for my PhD at Lancaster University and taught Religion and Education at St Mary's University , Twickenham. I co-authored *Love and Meaning in Religious Education* (Oxford University Press, 1984). My greatest achievement was the home-schooling of my three extraordinary children who share my vision, each in their own way.'

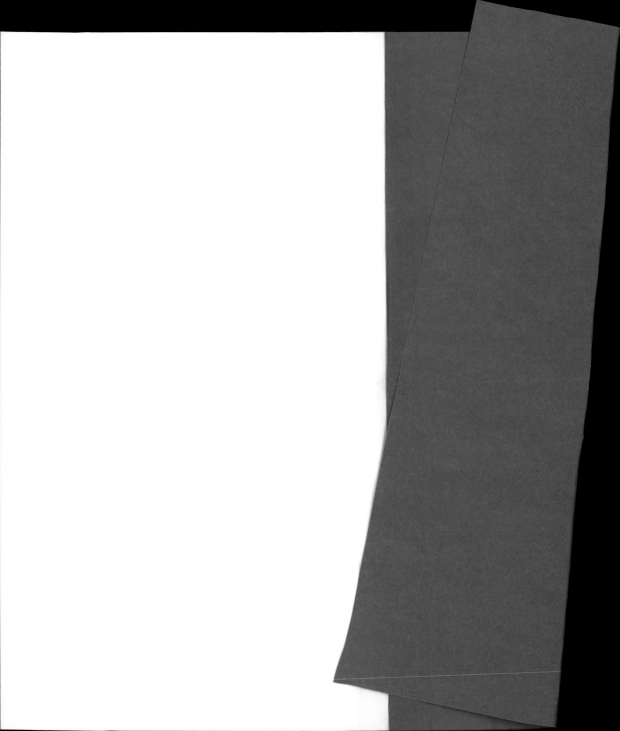